THIS BOOK CONSISTS OF 2 SEC
1. The first, with 20 color-coded songs
(pictured on the book cover).

2. The second has the "3 Little Pigs" fairy tale with a musical score. We suggest
a lot of activities that can be done with any percussion instrument or any sound
made with home utensils, for example, while listening to the story. This fairy tale
encourages a child's musical activity, even if they have never played music before.

20 XYLOPHONE SONGS AND MELODIES
Beginner Xylophone Sheet Music

This book was written to help an absolute beginner, whether child or adult,
learn to play the xylophone in a simple and easy way that requires no
knowledge of reading music. Just by following the color circles, you will
sound like an experienced musician. Playing music can be as simple and
enjoyable as a game. That is our goal: to give you what's necessary to
play beautiful music while having fun.

For good sound, it is necessary to learn to freely hold the mallets, and to
strike the keys of the xylophone lightly, aiming for the center of each key.
This percussion instrument develops not only hearing, but also gross and fine
motor skills, and cognitive skills such as letter recognition, matching,
and patterns.

All melodies in this book were written especially for this xylophone
and use the colors of its keys accordingly.
For some melodies, we group the circles to show the rhythm.
Some melodies which are played using more than 1-octave,
need to be played by ear.

Small circles or a particular color represent
the small key of that color on the xylophone,
while large circles represent the large keys.
Note that there are three sizes for
the light blue key, but only the
first two are used in the music.
Hitting a key represented by the mark #
inside the circle activates notes
on the upper row.

We put the melodies in the order
from simple to complex.

Recommended for ages 3 and up.

Most songs are played within this octave

Contents

Hot Cross Buns

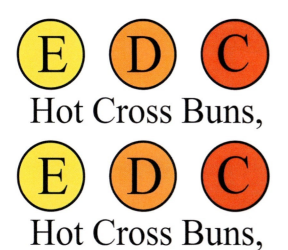

Hot Cross Buns,

Hot Cross Buns,

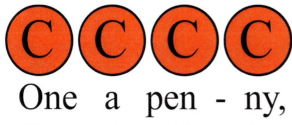

One   a   pen - ny,

two   a   pen - ny,

Hot Cross Buns

Hot Cross Buns,
Hot Cross Buns,
One a penny,
two a penny,
Hot Cross Buns

Are You Sleeping?

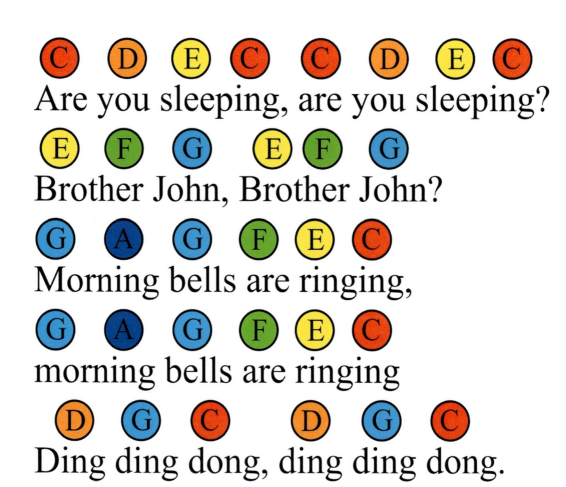

C D E C   C D E C
Are you sleeping, are you sleeping?

E F G   E F G
Brother John, Brother John?

G A G F E C
Morning bells are ringing,

G A G F E C
morning bells are ringing

D G C   D G C
Ding ding dong, ding ding dong.

Are you sleeping, are you sleeping?
Brother John, Brother John?
Morning bells are ringing,
morning bells are ringing
Ding ding dong, ding ding dong.

Mary Had A Little Lamb

E D C D E E E
Mary had a little lamb

D D D E G G
Little lamb, little lamb

E D C D E E E
Mary had a little lamb

E D D E D C
Its fleece was white as snow

Mary had a little lamb
Little lamb, little lamb
Mary had a little lamb
Its fleece was white as snow

The Wheels On The Bus

The wheels on the bus go round and round.

Round and round.Round and round.

The wheels on the bus go round and round.

Round and round.

The wheels on the bus go round and round.
Round and round.Round and round.
The wheels on the bus go round and round.
Round and round.

Twinkle, Twinkle Little Star

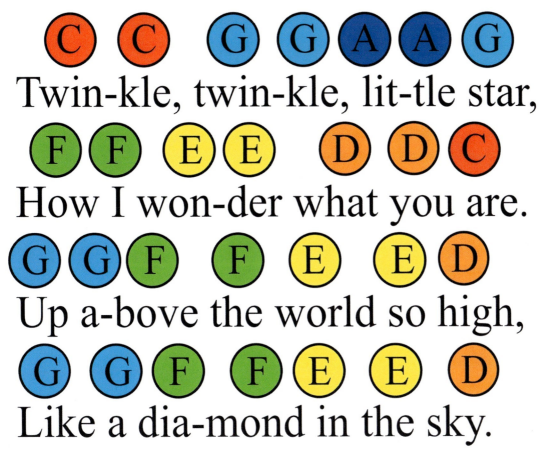

(C) (C) (G) (G) (A) (A) (G)

Twin-kle, twin-kle, lit-tle star,

(F) (F) (E) (E) (D) (D) (C)

How I won-der what you are.

(G) (G) (F) (F) (E) (E) (D)

Up a-bove the world so high,

(G) (G) (F) (F) (E) (E) (D)

Like a dia-mond in the sky.

Twinkle, twinkle, little star,
How I wonder what you are.
Up above the world so high,
Like a diamond in the sky.

5

Old MacDonald Had A Farm

(G) (G) (G) (D) (E) (E) (D) (B)(B)(A)(A)(G)
Old McDonald had a farm. E-I-E-I-O.
(D) (G) (G) (G) (D) (E) (E) (D)
And on that farm he had a cow.

(B)(B)(A)(A)(G)
E-I-E-I-O.

(D) (D) (G) (G) (G)
With a moo moo here.
(D) (D) (G) (G) (G)
With a moo moo here.
(G) (G) (G)
Here a moo.
(G) (G) (G)
There a moo.
(G) (G) (G) (G) (G) (G)
Everywhere a moo moo.
(G) (G) (G)(D) (E) (E) (D) (B)(B)(A)(A)(G)
Old McDonald had a farm. E-I-E-I-O.

What does a cow say?
Meow?
Oink?
Moo?

Do You Know The Muffin Man?

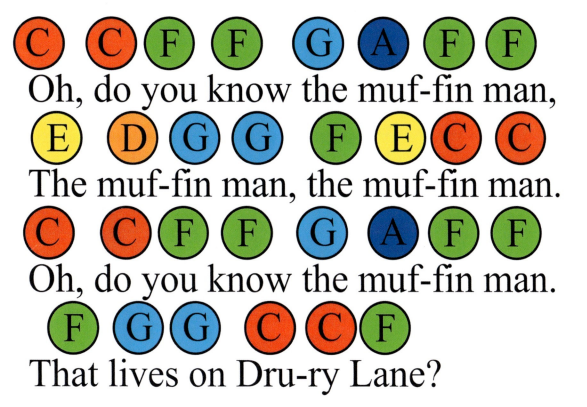

C C F F G A F F

Oh, do you know the muf-fin man,

E D G G F E C C

The muf-fin man, the muf-fin man.

C C F F G A F F

Oh, do you know the muf-fin man.

F G G C C F

That lives on Dru-ry Lane?

Oh, do you know the muffin man,
The muffin man, the muffin man.
Oh, do you know the muffin man.
That lives on Drury Lane?

London Bridge is Falling Down

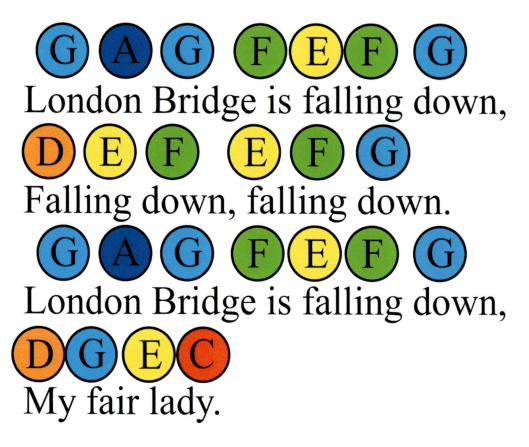

G A G F E F G

London Bridge is falling down,

D E F E F G

Falling down, falling down.

G A G F E F G

London Bridge is falling down,

D G E C

My fair lady.

London Bridge is falling down,
Falling down, falling down.
London Bridge is falling down,
My fair lady.

Jingle Bells

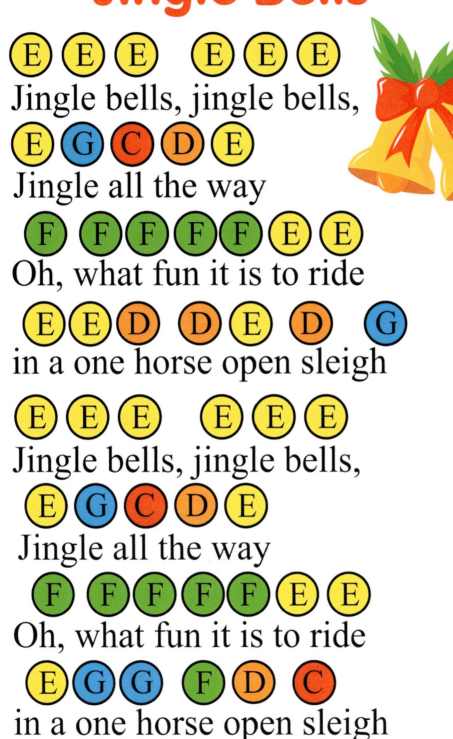

(E) (E) (E) (E) (E) (E)
Jingle bells, jingle bells,

(E) (G) (C) (D) (E)
Jingle all the way

(F) (F) (F) (F) (F) (E) (E)
Oh, what fun it is to ride

(E) (E) (D) (D) (E) (D) (G)
in a one horse open sleigh

(E) (E) (E) (E) (E) (E)
Jingle bells, jingle bells,

(E) (G) (C) (D) (E)
Jingle all the way

(F) (F) (F) (F) (F) (E) (E)
Oh, what fun it is to ride

(E) (G) (G) (F) (D) (C)
in a one horse open sleigh

We Wish You a Merry Christmas

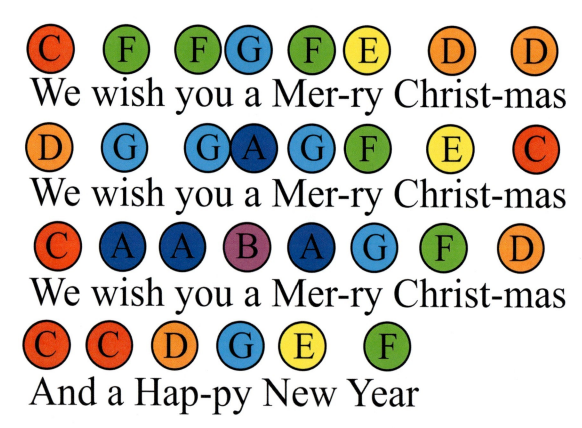

C F F G F E D D
We wish you a Mer-ry Christ-mas

D G G A G F E C
We wish you a Mer-ry Christ-mas

C A A B A G F D
We wish you a Mer-ry Christ-mas

C C D G E F
And a Hap-py New Year

We wish you a Merry Christmas
We wish you a Merry Christmas
We wish you a Merry Christmas
And a Happy New Year

10

Brahms's Lullaby
(Lullaby and Goodnight)

(E) (E)(G) (E) (E) (G)

Lullaby, and good night,

(E) (G) (C)(B) (A) (A) (G)

With pink roses bedight,

(D) (E)(F)(D) (D) (E) (F)

With lilies o'er spread,

(D) (F) (B)(A) (G) (B) (C)

Is my baby's sweet head.

(C) (C) (C) (A) (F) (G)

Lay you down now, and rest,

(E) (C) (F) (G) (A) (G)

May your slumber be blessed!

(C) (C) (C) (A) (F) (G)

Lay you down now, and rest,

(E) (C) (F) (E) (D) (C)

May your slumber be blessed!

Ode to Joy

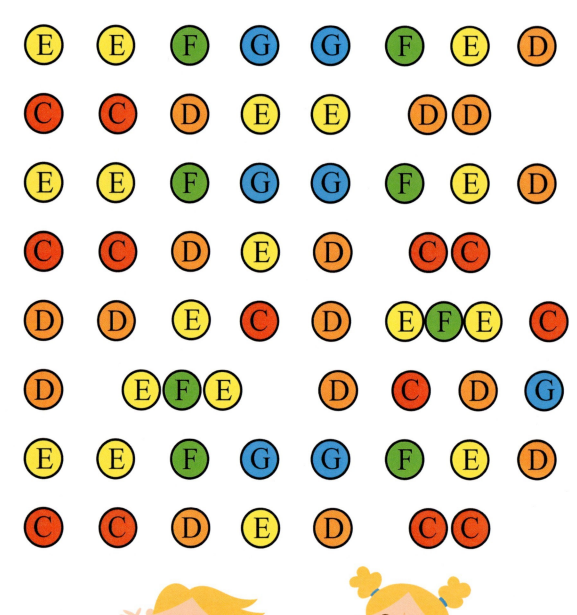

12

Happy Birthday

C C D   C F E

Happy birthday to you

C C D   C G F

Happy birthday to you

C C C   A F F E D

Happy birthday dear Mary

A# A# A   F G F

Happy birthday to you

Happy birthday to you
Happy birthday to you
Happy birthday dear Mary
Happy birthday to you

13

La Cucaracha

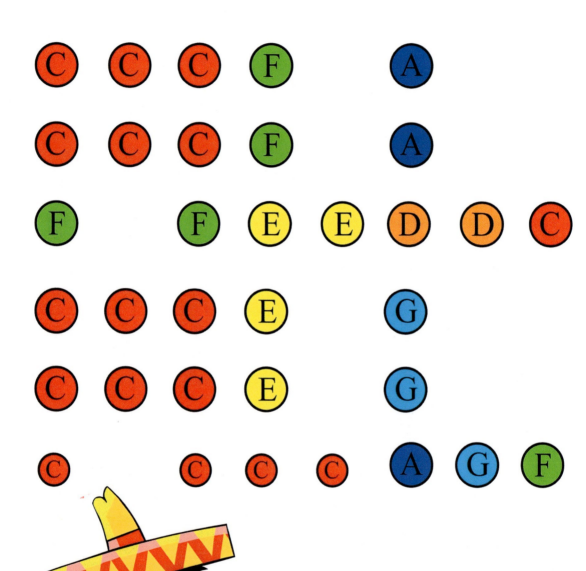

Oh! Susannah

Oh! I come from A-la-ba-ma

With my ban-jo on my knee

I'm going to Louis-i-a-na

My true love for to see.

Oh! Su-san-nah,

Don't you cry for me

I come from A-la-ba-ma

With my Ban-jo on my knee

Oh! I come from Alabama
With my banjo on my knee
I'm going to Louisiana
My true love for to see.
Oh! Susannah,
Don't you cry for me
I come from Alabama
With my Ban-jo on my knee

Beethoven - For Elise

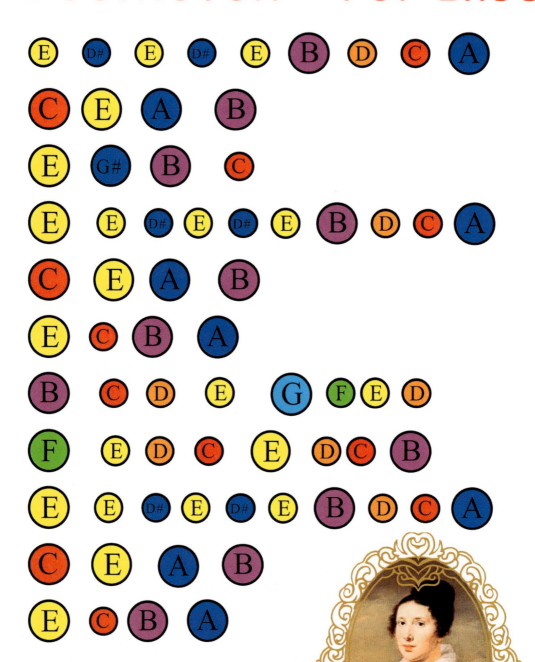

Silent Night

Silent night, holy night

All is calm, all is bright

Round yon Virgin Mother and Child

Holy Infant so tender and mild

Sleep in heavenly peace

Sleep in heavenly peace

Silent night, holy night
All is calm, all is bright
Round yon Virgin Mother and Child
Holy Infant so tender and mild
Sleep in heavenly peace
Sleep in heavenly peace

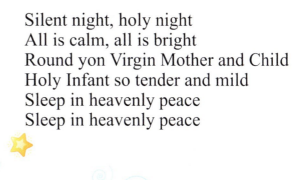

Now you have reached the level where you can play with letter notation. Some notes in these songs will be played not only within the main octave. The picture of the note doesn't reflect the key size and you will need to select the proper note by ear.

Yankee Doodle

Ⓒ Ⓒ Ⓓ Ⓔ Ⓒ Ⓔ Ⓓ
Yankee Doodle went to town

Ⓒ Ⓒ Ⓓ Ⓔ Ⓒ Ⓑ
riding on a pony,

Ⓒ   Ⓒ Ⓓ Ⓔ Ⓕ Ⓔ   Ⓓ
Stuck a feather in his cap

Ⓒ   Ⓑ   Ⓖ Ⓐ Ⓑ Ⓒ Ⓒ
And called it macaroni.

Ⓐ Ⓑ Ⓐ Ⓖ Ⓐ   Ⓑ Ⓒ
Yankee Doodle keep it up,

Ⓖ Ⓐ Ⓖ Ⓕ Ⓔ Ⓖ
Yankee Doodle dandy,

Ⓐ   Ⓑ Ⓐ Ⓖ Ⓐ Ⓑ   Ⓒ
Mind the music and the step,

Ⓐ   Ⓖ   Ⓒ   Ⓑ   Ⓓ Ⓒ Ⓒ
And with the girls be handy.

Yankee Doodle went to town
A-riding on a pony,
Stuck a feather in his cap
And called it macaroni.

Yankee Doodle keep it up,
Yankee Doodle dandy,
Mind the music and the step,
And with the girls be handy.

Row, Row, Row Your Boat

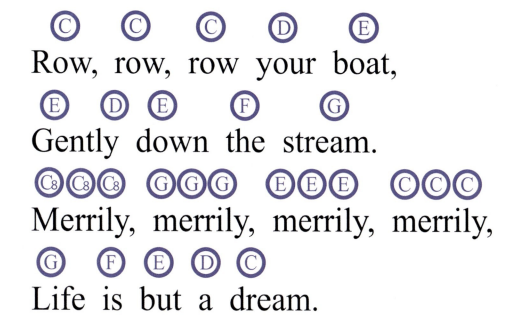

C   C   C   D   E
Row, row, row your boat,

E   D   E   F   G
Gently down the stream.

C8 C8 C8   G G G   E E E   C C C
Merrily, merrily, merrily, merrily,

G   F   E   D   C
Life is but a dream.

Row, row, row your boat,
Gently down the stream.
Merrily, merrily, merrily, merrily,
Life is but a dream.

Jolly Old Saint Nicholas

Ⓐ Ⓐ Ⓐ Ⓐ Ⓖ Ⓖ Ⓖ
Jolly old Saint Nicholas,
Ⓕ Ⓕ Ⓕ Ⓕ Ⓐ
Lean your ear this way.
Ⓓ Ⓓ Ⓓ Ⓓ Ⓒ Ⓒ Ⓕ
Don't you tell a single soul
Ⓖ Ⓕ Ⓖ Ⓐ Ⓖ
What I'm going to say.
Ⓐ Ⓐ Ⓐ Ⓐ Ⓖ Ⓖ Ⓖ
Christmas Eve is coming soon.
Ⓕ Ⓕ Ⓕ Ⓕ Ⓐ
Now, you dear old man,
Ⓓ Ⓓ Ⓓ Ⓓ Ⓒ Ⓒ Ⓕ
Whisper what you'll bring to me.
Ⓖ Ⓕ Ⓖ Ⓐ Ⓕ
Tell me if you can.

Jolly old St. Nicholas,
Lean your ear this way.
Don't you tell a single soul
What I'm going to say.
Christmas Eve is coming soon.
Now, you dear old man,
Whisper what you'll bring to me.
Tell me if you can.

THE THREE LITTLE PIGS, WITH MUSICAL SCORE

21

Onomatopoeia develops children's creative imagination, and introduces skills for playing percussion musical instruments. Children learn to adjust the volume and strength of sounds, enhance their listening skills, and develop their gross and fine motor skills. If several children are playing, they learn to wait their turn and develop patience. While reading the fairy tale, all music instruments should be easily accessible (i.e., lay out in front of or around the kids). For the first time, an adult should read the story and play the instrument by themself, with the kids only listening. Later, if the child is small, you can divide the instruments, giving kids only some of them for musical scoring. Later, the kids can play all the instruments, and even recite the whole fairy tale and score themselves. Encourage the kids if they suggest their own method of scoring or their own plot of the fairy tale.

The book was written using the Carl Orff approach. Orff believed that each child should not be a passive listener, but an active co-creator. He/she must have the opportunity to act and dance to accompany a composition and improvise while listening to or learning to play music. With this book you can be your kids' Orff music instructor, who encourages a child's natural sense of music, even if they have never played music before.

tambourine

maracas

green sleigh bell

pandeira

triangle

castanets

rattle with 3 bells

xylophone

eggs

23

Create sounds:

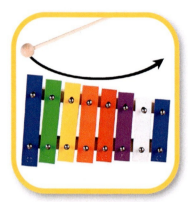

Slide the mallet along
all the notes of the xylophone

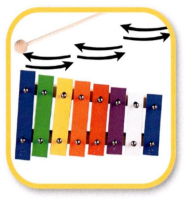

Slide the mallet back
and forth along 2-3 notes
on the xylophone

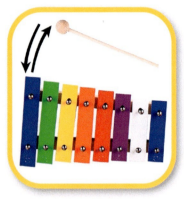

Hit note C several times

Hit note A several times

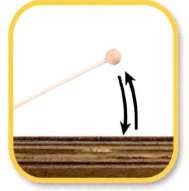

Knock the mallet
on table

Shake pandeira

Shake tambourine

Hit tambourine on table

Shake the eggs

24

Hit the triangle

Shake the rattle with 3 bells

Shake the green sleigh bell

Shake the maracas

Click the castanets

Rustle the polybag

Make growl sounds

Make howl sounds

Make blow sounds

THE THREE LITTLE PIGS

There once were 3 little pigs.

They were small and very merry *(pandeira shaking)*,

playing in their wonderful place by the river

(shaking tambourine).

It was summer and they frolicked in the sun and had

a wonderful time running *(xylophone sound slowly from G to G)*,

swimming *(xylophone splashes)*

and playing in the sand *(shaking eggs).*

One morning, they heard a knock on a tree *(castanets knocks)*.

They looked up and saw a woodpecker. The woodpecker asked them

where they were going to spend the winter because it was

getting colder. The carefree pigs hadn't thought about winter.

They continued to sing, *(shaking pandeira)*

and danced

(shaking tambourine)

and play together the rest of the day. *(3 bells rattle shaking)*

Several days later they heard a sleigh bell.

(green sleigh bell sound).

They looked up and saw a horse with a

cart passing by. The horse asked them

where they were going to stay over the

winter, which was upon them.

The happy-go-lucky piggies had

not made any plans yet.

It was only when it became colder, the rain began to come

very often *(beat 3 times note A on the xylophone)*

and they heard the Wolf UUUU in the forest *(howl sound)*

one morning that they began to build a home for the winter. The first

little pig was lazy and didn't want to work hard,

so he built his house out of straw *(rustle by polybag)*

very quickly. The second little pig worked a little bit harder:

he broke branches from the trees *(castanets sound)*

and built his house out of sticks. Then, they sang *(shaking pandeira)*

and danced *(shaking tambourine)*

and played together the rest of the day.

(3 bells rattle shaking)

The third little pig worked hard for several days.

He took some sand from the river *(maracas sounds)*

and stirred it with water *(eggs sounds)*

to make some bricks.

He built his house with the bricks, carefully

placing them one by one *(knock the mallet by the table)*.

It was a sturdy house complete with a fine fireplace and chimney.

It looked like it could withstand the strongest winds. He was very tired at

the end of the day, but very satisfied.

But the next day he sang *(shaking pandeira)*

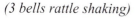

and danced *(shaking tambourine)*

and played with

his brothers for the rest of the day.

(3 bells rattle shaking)

A week later, a wolf happened to pass by the lane where the three little

pigs lived; he saw the straw house, and he smelled the pig inside.

So he knocked on the door *(castanets sound)*,

rang in the doorbell *(triangle sound)*

and said:

RRRR *(growl sounds)*

«Little pig! Little pig! Let me in! Let me in!»

But the little pig saw the Wolf's big paws through the keyhole,

so he answered back:

«No! No! No! *(Hit small note C on the xylophone)*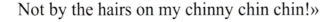

Not by the hairs on my chinny chin chin!»

Then the Wolf showed his teeth and said:

«Then I'll huff and I'll puff and I'll blow your house

down». So he huffed and he puffed and he blew

the house down!

(green sleigh bell sound).

The Wolf opened his jaws very wide,

he snapped his teeth very loud *(castanets sound)*

and bit down as hard as he could *(knock hand on table),*

but the first little pig escaped and

ran away very quickly *(xylophone C to C)*

to hide in the house of the second little pig and closed the door just near

the Wolf's nose

(hit tambourine on table).

The Wolf knocked on the door *(castanets sound),*

rang the doorbell *(triangle sound)*

and said: RRRR

(growl sounds)

«Little pigs! Little pigs! Let me in! Let me in!»

But the little pigs saw the Wolf's pointy ears through the keyhole, so they

answered back: «No! No! No! *(hit small note C on the xylophone)*

Not by the hairs on our chinny chin chin!»

So the Wolf showed his teeth

and said: RRRR *(growl sounds)*

«Then I'll huff and I'll puff and I'll blow your house down».

So he huffed and he puffed and he blew

the house down! *(green sleigh bell sound)*.

The Wolf was greedy and he tried to catch both pigs at once,

but he was too greedy and got neither! His big

jaws clamped down on nothing *(castanets sound)*

but air and the two little pigs scrambled away as fast as

their little hooves would carry them. *(xylophone from C to C)*

The Wolf chased them down the lane and he almost caught them. But

they made it to the brick house and slammed the door closed just as the

Wolf's nose began to enter *(hit tambourine on table)*.

The three little pigs were very frightened. They

sat together and trembled with fear *(maracas sounds)*

because they knew the Wolf wanted to eat them.

And that was very, very true.

So he knocked on the door *(castanets sound)*,

rang the doorbell *(triangle sound)*

and said: RRRR

(growl sounds)

«Little pigs! Little pigs! Let me in! Let me in!»

But the little pigs saw the Wolf's narrow eyes through the keyhole, so they

answered back: «No! No! No! *(hit note C on the xylophone)*

Not by the hairs on our chinny chin chin!»

So the Wolf showed his teeth *(castanets knock)*

and said: «Then I'll huff and I'll puff and I'll blow your house down». Well!

He huffed and he puffed *(blow)*.

He puffed and he huffed *(shaking maracas)*.

And he huffed, huffed *(rustling of packages)*,

and he puffed, puffed; *(green sleigh bell sound)*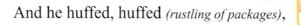

but he could not blow the house down.

At last, he was so out of breath that he couldn't huff and he

couldn't puff anymore. So he stopped to rest and thought a bit.

Then he climbed on to the roof and even the roof shook *(shake eggs)*

and he jumped down the chimney. At that time, the piglets

were cooking soup. Water was boiling in a pot *(shake maracas)*

on the fire. Then, just as the Wolf was coming down the chimney,

the little piggy pulled off the lid, and plop! in *(hit triangle)*

fell the Wolf into the scalding water. Another little

pig opened the door at that time.

The Wolf howled, shook himself off and run out the door and

disappeared into the woods.

The little pig shut the door *(knock the mallet)*.

And then the 3 little pigs sang *(shaking pandeira)*

and danced *(shaking tambourine)*

and played together

for the rest of the day. *(3 bells rattle shaking)*.

They decided to live

together, never be lazy

and help each other.

Made in the USA
Coppell, TX
12 December 2020